Beautiful Lighthouses Coloring Book

Collection of Hand Drawn Seaside Landscape Sketches for Adults

Rachel Mintz

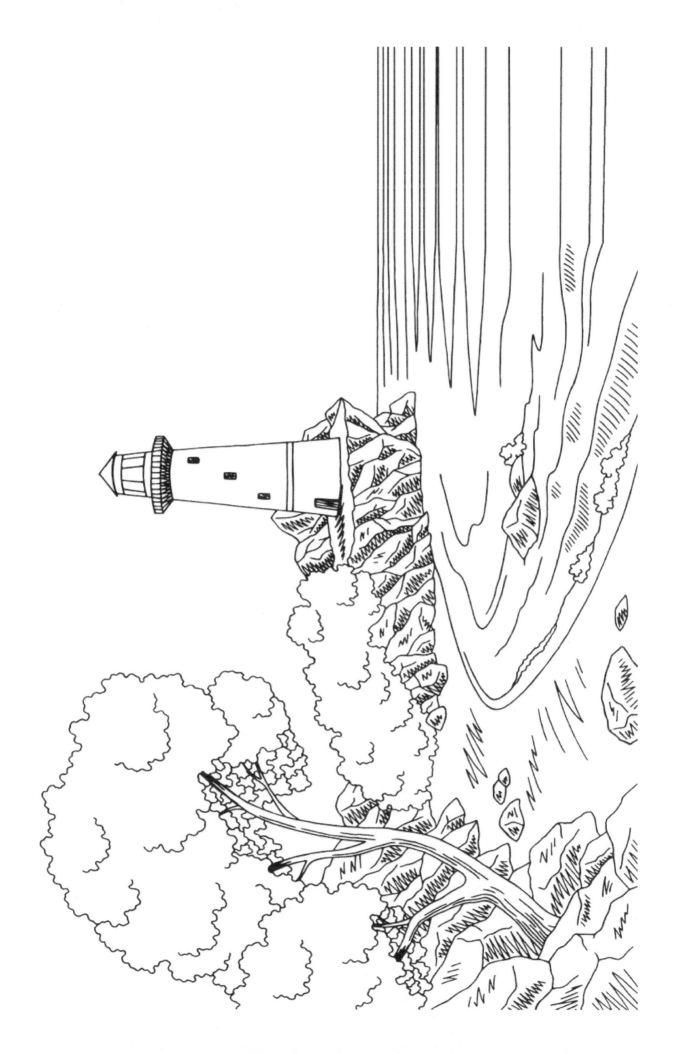

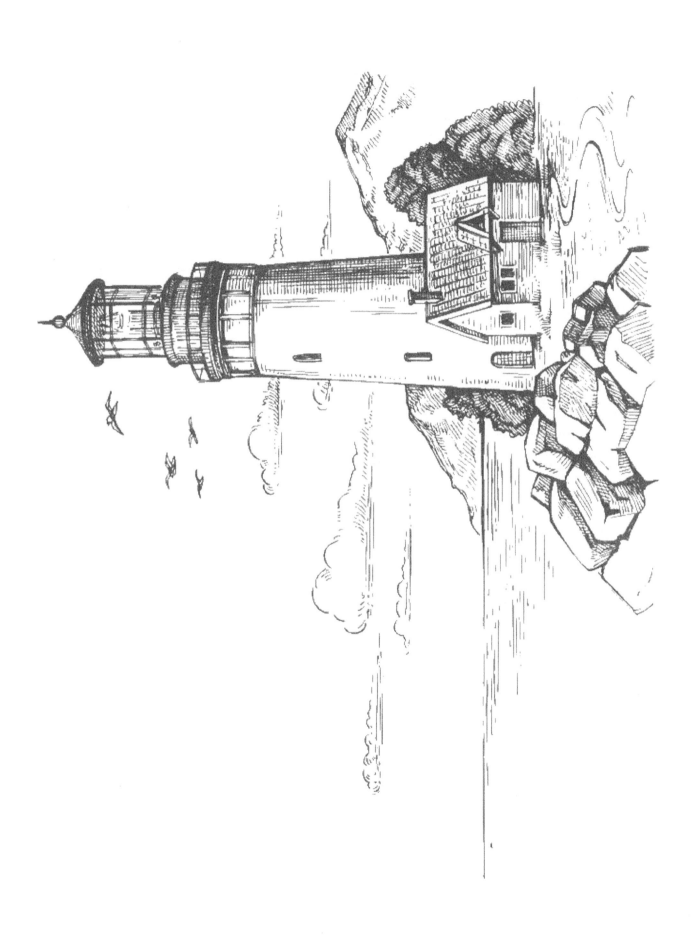

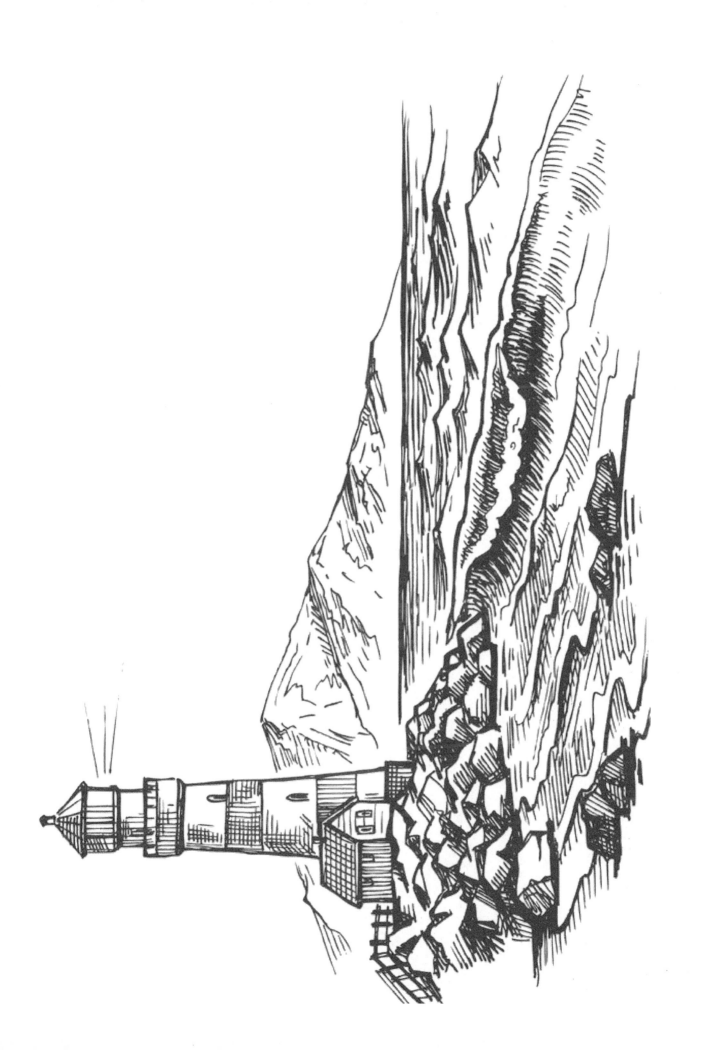

Thank you for coloring with us!

Enjoy some bonus pages from our coloring books:

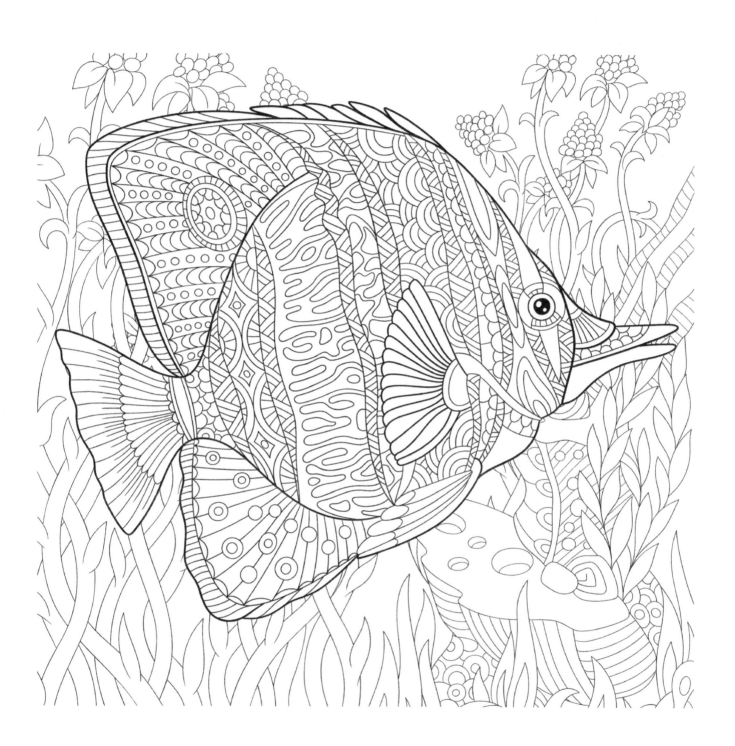

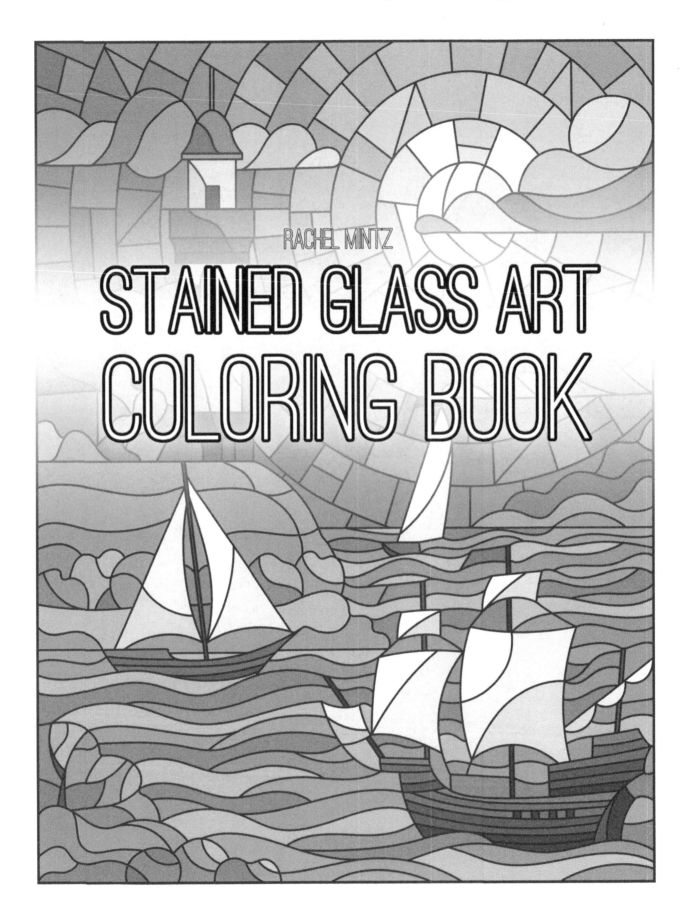

NEW Coloring book at Amazon, have fun with it...

Did you have fun with this book?
Let everyone know! Add a review at Amazon!

Made in the USA
Middletown, DE
06 March 2023

26286060R00044